Pure Love

Affirmations just for this moment ...

Carole A. Daxter

H J KRAMER INC
Tiburon, California

H J Kramer Inc
P.O. Box 1082
Tiburon, CA 94920

Library of Congress Cataloging-in-Publication Data

Daxter, Carole A.
    Pure love : affirmations just for this moment / by Carole Daxter.
        p.   cm.
    ISBN 0–915811–27–8 : $7.95
    1. Conduct of life.   2. Success.   3. Meditations.
4. Affirmations.   I. Title.
BJ1581.2.B359   1990
158′.1—dc20   90–52729
                                                              CIP

Editor: Nancy Grimley Carleton
Cover Art: Jeanette Stobie
Cover Design: Spectra Media
Composition by: Classic Typography
Book Production: Schuettge and Carleton

Manufactured in the United States of America

10   9   8   7   6   5   4   3   2   1

Acknowledgments

I thank my husband Brian for his continued support, encouragement, and unconditional love.

I thank the Universe for guiding all the right people into my life who have influenced me and helped me to grow.

I thank my family and friends. Just by being in my life, they have taught me so much.

I thank the following authors: Catherine Ponder, Colin P. Sisson, U. S. Anderson, Louise I. Hay, Robert A. Monroe, and Kahlil Gibran. In reading their material, I have expanded my knowledge, and this has enabled me to help others.

I thank my daughter, Tracy Kenworth, and her partner, Geoffrey Bickford, for their continued support and help regarding the graphics and layout of the books.

Special thanks to Wilma John, who partook in the task of proofreading and editing. Bless you, Wilma.

I thank you, the reader, for being my kindred spirit in the divine power of love.

I dedicate to you the prayer
of St. Francis of Assisi:

Lord, make me a channel of thy peace,
That where there is hatred
I may bring love;
That where there is wrong
I may bring the spirit of forgiveness;
That where there is discord
I may bring harmony;
That where there is error
I may bring truth;
That where there is doubt
I may bring faith;
That where there is despair
I may bring hope;
That where there are shadows
I may bring thy light;
That where there is sadness
I may bring joy.

In time of need, run your fingers through the book and ask, "What is the affirmation for me today?" Where your finger stops is your answer.

Lord, grant that I may seek
Rather to comfort
Than to be comforted;
To understand
Than to be understood;
To love
Than to be loved;
For it is by giving
That one receives;
It is by self-forgetting
That one finds;
It is by forgiving
That one is forgiven;
It is by dying
That one awakens to eternal life.

Introduction

All too often we allow our thoughts and emotions to focus on what "has been" or what "might be" and forget about the importance of *this* moment.

We think and verbalize words of fear, resentment, hatred, criticism, power struggles, impatience, and so forth, when all we really need to do is change our thinking from our draining, emotional pattern, and simply focus on thoughts of love, peace, and tranquility.

The purpose of this book is to help us change our thoughts and words and become aware of the love within.

While holding the book, and focusing on thoughts of the moment, allow your fingers to run through the book. Where your finger stops is your answer. Read, reread, and reread again.

That is all we need to do; we have now focused our thoughts onto love. We can use the affirmation for today and continue daily until we feel the affirmation bcomes a natural expression of our lives in every moment.

I know my life changed when I affirmed daily beautiful, positive, loving words, changed from a life of despair, depression, and inner turmoil to one of faith, love, and peace of mind.

Please allow that part of you, that part of me, "the kindred spirit," to guide us on an inner journey of fulfillment.

This way, we'll see the old emotional trauma simply disappear and dissolve. Then we will experience joy, peace, tranquility, and harmony in this moment, which is eternity.

Who's Responsible?

All too often in society today, we find it a challenge to live without stressful, emotional actions. We find it difficult, because we have placed that pressure on ourselves. No event, no one, does it to us. We only do it to ourselves.

For so long, we have readily blamed external forces, such as God, the devil, parents, teachers, society, the weather, and so on. This is because we've been conditioned to think that way.

Then there is the fear that if we say to ourselves, "I brought this trauma into my life," we will be totally alone and unable to muster the strength to carry on. Rightly so, for our patterned thinking and beliefs have led us to believe we always need support and reassurance from the external. And why not? We've been getting it for years. We've always had reassurance one way or another, whether it be in a negative put-down or the positive pickup.

So, how can we alleviate the stress? How can we free ourselves of fear? How can we show love without hurt? How can we be healthy? How can we be happy? How can we be successful? How can we be free from stressful, emotional trauma?

It's simple — change the way we are thinking. It's that easy!

The reason it is that easy is because we are all created in the same powerful source — pure love. Call it God, Spirit, Divine Love, the Universe, or the power within. Call it whatever you like. The same powerful, unconditional love is within us all, and it is our birthright to dwell in it.

This power vibrates on a frequency that we have buried away and therefore we are not always able to recognize it in ourselves or others. Perhaps we think that we don't even possess it. We do. Each and every one of us all have that same power — pure love. So to trigger off this beautiful power within us, we need to relearn and reprogram ourselves with good, positive, loving, peaceful thoughts and words. These thoughts and words will filter to the truth, the love within, and allow us to become that power totally. Gradually, our pattern of thinking becomes our reality and it feels good. It is good!

We are experiencing a form of "rebirth." We are recognizing, learning, and understanding a different perception from what we have been conditioned to believe.

The Power of Thoughts and Words

Did you know that you are a very powerful person on this planet — powerful in every sense of the word? For with every thought, with every word, you are creating your life, creating your world.

The time has come to be in a state of awareness that allows us to recognize the true power we hold in our minds. While this power has always been with us, it's an exciting time now, for now more than ever before our awareness is being brought into focus on just what this power is. When we look at our lives, we see that there is rarely a moment that we are not thinking or verbalizing thoughts and words. This takes up ninety-eight percent of our time. So, here lies the power: Each thought and each word verbalized, whether it is negative or positive, creates our life.

When we are prepared to accept the challenge to change our thinking and use this power wisely, we benefit ourselves and the world. I say we benefit the world, for when we change our thoughts and change our words so that they are explicitly always of love, then the world will change accordingly.

Now, this moment, is the time to look at our thinking. What are we thinking right now? Are we thinking, "Nothing's going right"? Are we thinking, "I'm sick and tired of work"? Are our thoughts filled with fear, anguish, and resentment? Or are they thoughts of peace, love, and tranquility? Let's look at what we *are* thinking now! If what we are thinking is negative, then we must simply redirect our thoughts onto what we wish for ourselves and others, in a loving way. For what we focus on constantly in our thoughts is stored in our aura, which then vibrates in pure energy and sends impulses into the Universe. Like magnets, these thoughts then attract into our lives what we have been thinking and believing. Irrespective of whether this is positive or negative, we attract people and events to us that we don't always recognize as having emanated from our own subconscious choice and doing.

Our trained logical thinking and eyes present us with so-called "evidence" of what is happening in our lives. We then worry about it (especially if we perceive it to be bad), dwell on it in our thoughts and words, and dwell on it with strong emotions. All this then creates similar circumstances over and over again.

If we view these situations as something we can learn from, we can start *now* with affirmations to bring about a change from our old patterned thinking.

Change is all around us, but we constantly balk at changing ourselves. We think this is not possible, for we have all too often felt far too comfortable in laying blame on the outside world, blaming others for our situations and life as we are experiencing it!

Some of us are afraid that if we stop laying blame on the external, we will then have to start with ourselves. Surely, if we wish to live on a planet filled with love, peace, and harmony, we do need to start with ourselves, and stop waiting for someone else to do it.

So let's change now and live in the kingdom of heaven God promised. "Heaven" simply means harmony, so *we can* experience heaven right now.

What Are Affirmations?

An affirmation is merely a group of words put together to make a sentence. That sentence is the affirmation. Let us choose these words with care, for these words create our reality.

So let's think carefully about what we want in our lives. Let us be precise! Let us understand what we are affirming. For instance, "I am prosperity" is a fantastic affirmation, but what does it mean? Does it mean an abundance in everything? Does it mean an abundance in just one area? Prosperity means different things to different people. I found at the beginning of my growth work that I needed to affirm exactly what I wanted to prosper in. I affirmed, "I prosper in love. I prosper in good health. I prosper in financial areas." Finally, I could say, "I am prosperity," and *know that I am.*

With these words, we *create* a state of mind; then we *experience* what we have set in motion with our thoughts and words.

Why Do Affirmations Work?

We are all created from the same source—pure love. Through past experiences, we may not recognize that we are all conceived "in love," but we are. The Bible says, "In the beginning was the word, the word was God, and God is love." We were created in God's image; therefore, we were created in "love."

In our years of acquiring learned knowledge, clamoring for "something better," we have simply stifled and blocked our awareness to the beautiful, simple, basic power of love. By using affirmations, we are making a pathway to the Divine Love within. Affirmations are a triggering device, releasing that Divine Love to the surface, where we can experience it consciously, physically, and spiritually. The more we use affirmations, the more positive and aware of this love we become.

Remember, whatever we focus on in our thoughts and words is stored in our aura and, in turn, becomes a powerful magnet.

How to Use Affirmations

Repetition is the key. "Practice makes perfect" is an old saying that is most apt for affirmations. For in the practicing and the repetition, we are reprogramming ourselves so that old negative beliefs may be released once and for all.

Write affirmations over and over again. Remember the lines we wrote at school? Once a school teacher came to see me, and after consultation I suggested to her that she write one hundred lines. I suggested that her lines be "I am prosperity," one hundred times every day for a week! With a bit of a smirk, off she went. Three weeks later, she rang me and thanked me for the "homework," for she excitedly exclaimed, "I've just scratched off $10,000 in an instant lottery. I'll recommend your lines to everyone!"

I recommend this method of writing affirmations over and over again. It brings results! The physical impact with written affirmations is that we see what we are writing, and the retina then continues registering, sending impulses into our subconscious, where the affirmation is stored and remembered for continual use.

We are all individuals; therefore, I suggest that we write the affirmations for as long as we feel comfortable in any one sitting. Comfort is the key, especially when we first start using affirmations daily. Impatience can creep in (it did with me).

Write affirmations onto different colored cards. Put the colored cards on your mirror or somewhere visible where you will see them first thing in the morning. Each card is a reminder to start your day with peaceful, loving thoughts. Also, when we see the particular color during the day, it triggers off automatically the affirmation on that card. Have affirmations available so that you can read them and say them before going to bed, for "affirmation" is another word for prayer. Before long, you will have developed a routine of using affirmations daily.

The power of the spoken word is a useful tool with affirmations. Shout them, sing them, say them—whatever takes your fancy. The power lies with the vibration sent through our body each time we utter a sound. The impact is doubled, for we hear our words as well. With this vibration, we can then *feel* the affirmations working. We will notice that we feel free from worry, that we feel more alive.

Recording affirmations on tape is an easy method

I have found. Research has shown and proven that recorded affirmations that are played back while sleeping are actually received by the subconscious. The subconscious receives the message loud and clear; the individual awakens refreshed and feeling wonderful. Playing your tapes while you drive is also beneficial.

What if some of the old negative thoughts creep in during the day? The key is: Don't give up! Let's remember, "Inch by inch, it's a cinch; yard by yard, it's a bit hard." So, too, with affirmations. In the beginning, we might experience a little difficulty; we could even want to give up. We must *believe* that affirmations will wash away the negative beliefs. This is the moment to train ourselves not to react, but simply to respond with loving thoughts and affirmations. After a while, we will find there is no need to feel frustrated, angry, or rejected, because we will know the affirmations are working. Then we will be operating in Divine Love. Let us affirm daily, "I am always at the right place at the right time, every moment of my life, successfully doing the right thing."

Affirmations allow us to focus on this very moment, for this is the only moment ever with us. Too often we concern ourselves with yesterday and tomorrow; in so doing, we forget about the *now*. We forget that it is *now* and that we are creating a wonderful, eternal *now*.

There is really nothing new about affirmations; the challenge is to try them and see what happens in your world. Say the affirmations; feel the affirmations—then the affirmation *is* you.

In our growth work, after using affirmations for a while, we feel good about ourselves and sometimes forget to continue using them. I see great benefits daily in remembering to use affirmations.

We can start each day with affirmations:

"Good morning, Universe. I happily greet this day with excitement, for I am happy to be alive. I give thanks, for today is complete and unfolds to me miraculous, wondrous things. This day is perfect for me" (quoted from *Love and Peace Through Affirmation*).

We can bring love into our life by affirming, "I am loving to myself, and I express Divine Love fully."

We can bring good health into our lives with the affirmation "I am always in perfect good health. My body is healthy and I feel better and better every day in every way."

We can use affirmations to bring riches into our lives: "I achieve all things successfully and bring great riches into my life under grace in a perfect way."

And so it goes on. We can use affirmations to bring everything we require and desire into our lives. Again, the Bible says, "Ask and you will receive," and indeed we do. However, we don't always want the things when we get them. So, in using affirmations, the power is that we learn to know what is true for us. We learn to change our perceptions and not attach emotional trauma to our thinking. We simply learn love of the unconditional kind.

Join with me now and affirm daily, "Divine Love fills my life; Divine Love fills my being; Divine Love prospers me and is in every situation now." See what happens!

Let us start now to rekindle the Divine Love within each and every one of us. Then we will see ourselves, our relationships, and the world in love, peace, and harmony. Take care of yourself and be gentle with yourself, for you are beautiful and unique; you are a perfect creation of Divine Love.

By using affirmations, we can learn to live "just for this moment." For it is this minute, the one we are experiencing, which is all-important. When we focus thoughts on love, peace, forgiveness, harmony, and happiness in *this moment,* we are then assured that this moment is eternity!

The most powerful things in the Universe are thoughts; choose them with care and dwell in your birthright of Divine Love.

The Affirmations

just for this moment ...

I see that
I learn
strength
from every
situation
in my
life.

AFFIRM
DAILY.

just for this moment ...

I seek not to blame, and I
release the feelings of failure. There
is no separation in the eyes of the God
within, for we are all from the same source—
Divine Love. All my life's experiences are
my teachers, and I am a willing student.
When I learn worthiness and self-respect,
I know I will attract beautiful loving
relationships into my life. I express
my life with unconditional
love.

I am strength.

I
am at
one with
the pure
essence
of life.

AFFIRM
DAILY.

just for this moment ...

*I see that love still dwells
within, though the bodies cannot
be together. In the kingdom of heaven,
there can be no separation. It is only my
perception, my beliefs, and my yearning that
see separation. When I recognize the true
God flow within, I know then that love
is all there is. I will feel no separation,
only wholeness, completeness,
and simply being.*

I am at one.

I
know I
have an
endless
supply
of energy
to use.

AFFIRM
DAILY.

just for this moment...

I rest easy and relax in the knowledge that my Divine Source gives me all the energy I require. My short temper, anger, and frustrations disappear as I learn to listen to my body, which is a living temple of God. I rest and allow the God flow to nourish me and replenish my body with zeal so that I move through life easily and joyfully.

I am energy.

I fill
my being
with peace,
love, and
light, and this
touches
all I
meet.

AFFIRM
DAILY.

just for this moment ...

I see a Divine Loving Spirit
within a body of restrictions. I
know that to express and be at one
with the Divine Creator I only need to
use thoughts. Thoughts are a powerful tool
to create my life, and I create them with
love. It is not the body that projects
beauty; it is the Divine Love
within. I fill my aura with
peace, love, and light,
and it touches all I
meet in the
same way.

I am complete.

I
find
gentle and
compassionate
ways of
expressing
myself.

AFFIRM
DAILY.

just for this moment ...

I see that it is okay to be truthful. As I expand my awareness, I know I find gentle, compassionate ways to express myself easily. I totally accept myself. Therefore I seek no recognition, for I know the God within is kind, gentle, caring, and accepting at all times. I choose to reflect and express that compassion now.

I am expression.

I let
revenge
go and know
there is
harmony
in my life.

AFFIRM
DAILY.

just for this
moment . . .

I release the fear of being hurt.
I put love into life and that is what
I receive. The Divine Spirit within seeks
neither revenge nor justice; it is only my
perception that thinks this way. Peace and
harmony are my birthright, and I accept
this for myself now. In this acceptance,
I rest easy, knowing that all those
around me are searching for
joy, peace, and
love, too.

I am forgiving.

I respond
lovingly,
for I now
know I
exist only
in the
light of God.

AFFIRM
DAILY.

just for this
moment ...

*I fill my ego with love. My
ego is the prince of darkness that
has hindered my way to the light.
I now recognize all reactions are attached
to ego. I bless, I praise, and I give thanks, for
I know I am walking in the light when I
see the shadow behind me. I choose to
respond lovingly and harmoniously,
for I now know that I exist only
in the light of God—
and that is love.*

I am at one.

I
see
happiness
in passing
into the
care of
God.

AFFIRM
DAILY.

just for this moment ...

I see that in dying I now
learn what living is all about. I
do not see dying as a loss or separation
from loved ones. It is not something to fear,
for God promises eternal life for all, not
just a few. In death, the body merely
fades away, but the spirit lives on
and on. I now see joy in passing
from this time space to another,
which is a space of love, peace,
and harmony. I know the
love I feel will never die,
for love is eternal.

I am eternal life.

It is
my divine
birthright
to love
and be loved;
I happily
accept it
now.

AFFIRM
DAILY.

just for this moment...

*I see that I create my reality.
I now choose my divine birthright,
which is love. I happily recognize that
love is faith, which brings to me a bright
new beginning. I now choose this moment
to be a step toward fulfillment. It is my
divine birthright of love, which wants
me to understand, be loving, be
gentle on myself, and be free.*

I am life.

I am
always
at the
right place
successfully
doing the
right
thing.

AFFIRM
DAILY.

just for this moment ...

*I focus on all the events of
my life, no matter how small,
and see the achievements there.
The Divine Spirit within guides me
perfectly to the right place at the right
time. My pathway is a journey to knowledge
and releasing old thoughts and beliefs of
misfortune. I learn something new
from every experience, and this
allows me to live fully in
harmonious faith. Faith
brings me strength
and recognition
that success
is at hand.*

I am at peace.

I
see that
there is
joy in
living and
in loving.

AFFIRM
DAILY.

just for this moment ...

I see that there is so much to live for. There is no ending, only my perception. I need to learn love and know that I am worthy of giving and receiving that love. I pray for help and guidance and in the asking I receive. I now recognize that there is warmth, compassion, and understanding in life. I now choose to take life moment by moment, step by step, and to learn new courage, new hope, and fulfillment. I have everything to gain and nothing to lose.

I am loving life.

I
release
pity,
and I behold
this moment
with
wonder.

AFFIRM
DAILY.

just for this moment ...

I pity not lest I pity me. The
reflection I see all around only
reflects me. The creator of my world
is me, and I now see all is perfect as it
should be. I see each moment as a learning
experience, and I see with glee that there
is nothing to pity, nothing to judge,
simply to be. The love within is
a wonder to behold, and I am
full of that wonder.

I am full of wonder.

My
prosperity
is growing
every
day in
every way.

AFFIRM
DAILY.

just for this moment ...

*I lift my eyes to the heavens
above and see an abundance of
all things. I learn to release my feelings
of lack, for the Divine Creator loves me and
wants me to live life in abundance. I
grow and expand my knowledge to
understand that when I live in
the light of God I am rich. I
now choose to see the
abundance I have
around me and
I rejoice.*

I am prosperity.

I
bring
joy and
laughter
into my
life now.

AFFIRM
DAILY.

just for this moment ...

My heart is gladdened, for
this sadness will pass. I learn
easily to accept into my life happy,
joyous, exhilarating events that are rewarding
for me. I attach no emotions, for I have
no failure, no limitations, no lack in
any way. I express only tears of
joy, for I know I dwell in the
true essence of love, which
is true happiness.

I am laughter.

I see
joy and a new
beginning
in the
passing
of a soul
through
time.

AFFIRM
DAILY.

just for this moment ...

I grieve not, for I recognize
that the loving spirit lives on. I
honor the memory, and I now live life
in a more rewarding manner, knowing the
love within is, and always will be, with me.
I see joy in the passing of a soul, for it is
a birth, a new beginning. I am happy
for the soul passing through time,
which passes into the
safekeeping of God.

I am joyful.

I
am
always a
loving,
forgiving
person.

AFFIRM
DAILY.

just for this
moment ...

*I cannot change the
past, but I can certainly
learn from it now. I choose
to let go of the tired emotions
and judgments of yesterday. I
happily replace them with patience,
compassion, kindness, and peace. I feel
a sense of relief, a sense of joy, when true
forgiveness is achieved. I realize that
when there is forgiveness in my
heart I will then know my
yearning for love
is fulfilled.*

I am happily forgiving.

I now
choose
to be in
the quiet,
still
patience
of love.

AFFIRM
DAILY.

just for this moment ...

*I see that impatience springs
forth when I want things to happen
now! There is no need for me to worry,
to hurry, or to force events into my life,
because the Spirit knows what is for
my divine good. I now realize that
to learn patience is to allow my
life to flow with ease. The love
within is changeless and ever
constant, and I now choose
to be in that quiet, still,
patient love.*

I am patience.

I
dissolve
my hatred and
desire for revenge
in the pure
essence of
love.

AFFIRM
DAILY.

just for this moment ...

I release all judgments, all
hatred, all revenge. Imprisonment
is surrendering freedom in living. In
the knowledge that the power within
seeks only truth and wisdom, I see that
the divine laws of love will prevail.
My Spirit is forgiving, gentle, and
loving, and I now claim my
divine birthright, which
is a harmonious peace.

I am forgiving.

I
express
the pure
love of
the Spirit
within.

AFFIRM
DAILY.

just for this
moment ...

*I see that lust is the trappings
of sexual energy, all too often interpreted
as love. As I learn to grow and expand my
knowledge, I see that it is okay to
express myself lovingly. I express
the pure love of the Spirit
within, which is sensitive,
understanding, and
fulfilling in
every way.*

I am safe.

I
have
faith
that all
religious
pathways
lead to
God.

AFFIRM
DAILY.

just for this moment ...

I see God as love and religion as a way to find God. I see each religion as many people of many cultures trying to obtain love, peace, and harmony. I see that the divine God Spirit within allows me to travel whatever religious pathway I see as befitting me. God is love; God is light; God is peace. I now choose to dwell in that place and express that peace gently.

I am belief.

I
release the
feelings
of guilt
and betrayal,
because
I am loving
and forgiving.

AFFIRM
DAILY.

just for this moment ...

*I fill the moment with love.
I forgive: I release the feelings
of guilt and betrayal. The power
within does not condemn, does not
punish, but guides me to express love
and receive love in a nonsexual manner.
The power within is a gentle, pure love. I
constantly bless and praise the situation
and see that in total forgiveness there
is trust, love, and understanding,
which brings me
peace of mind.*

I am forgiveness.

I
release
all shame,
guilt, and
imbalance;
I am
perfect
right now.

AFFIRM
DAILY.

just for this moment ...

I release all shame, discord, imbalance, and guilt, for the God within does not recognize these. In my search for truth, I see that there is nothing to feel guilty about. It is only my perception that makes it so. I breathe in love and express that love endlessly in every situation of my life. The God within showers me with love and I choose to accept and recognize it is with me now.

I am balance.

I
grow and
learn to
understand
all things
perfectly.

AFFIRM
DAILY.

just for this moment ...

I see all the knowledge of
the Universe is mine to behold.
I release all misinterpretations that
I perceived according to what I felt was
true for me. I now expand my awareness
to learn that understanding comes from
within. The power within understands
all and springs forth now from the
well of love, which dwells within
me. I now choose and accept
this gentle love.

I am understanding.

God
is love,
and that
love is
my urge
to live.

AFFIRM
DAILY.

just for this moment...

*I see that "in the beginning
there was the word and the word was
God and God is Love." I was conceived
and born in love, and it is my perception
of what that love is that makes me the way
I am. I know I have that love within,
and I now choose to express it daily,
each moment in my life, and be free.
I lose all restrictions, I surrender
to the beauty, the wisdom, and
the truth, and I learn happily
what God is. God is love,
and that love is my
urge to live.*

I am love.

Your
words
have no
meaning;
I am full
of love
and light.

AFFIRM
DAILY.

just for this moment ...

"*Sticks and stones may break
my bones, but names can never
hurt me.*" It matters not what is
said or how it is spoken, for it is my
interpretation that invokes the pain. God
within fills me with peace and tranquility as
I grow to like and love myself. In this
growth, I realize I will hear words
uttered but they will bounce off
my shield of tranquility. God
within fills me with that
peaceful state of being
now, and I choose
words that reflect
that peace.

I am tranquil.

I am
still, and
I live
every
moment
in joy
and love.

AFFIRM
DAILY.

just for this moment ...

I see I only hurt myself in violence, for I seek punishment. I wish to change the feeling of unworthiness and break the pattern of hurting. The Spirit within knows no violence, only harmony. I sing songs of praise, for I know to change this violent world I need to change me. I choose to live every moment in joy and harmony. Then I know I am free.

I am worthy.

I
bring
order
into my
world
with
love.

AFFIRM
DAILY.

just for this
moment...

*I see that to bring order
into the world I must bring
order into my thinking. There
is only perfect harmony in the
Universe. The oceans, the valleys,
the mountains, the stars, and the planets
are all perfectly placed by the Creator of
life. I choose now with care to put my
thinking into order, so that I will
then experience perfection
in every moment.*

I am order.

I
am full
of love,
and my
pain is
released.

AFFIRM
DAILY.

just for this moment ...

I bless the pain, I praise
the pain, and I love the pain,
for in doing so I am able to release
all tension. I relax and focus only on
loving thoughts over and over and over
again, for then I am free. The Divine Spirit
realizes only love, which has no pain.
When I express only lovable words,
my Spirit lifts me. I excitedly
rejoice in the wisdom
of God.

I am peaceful.

I
have
faith,
and I live
only in
this
moment.

AFFIRM
DAILY.

just for this moment ...

I am filled with love
and courage. I see that
my old beliefs of haunting
tales and superstitions allowed
my imagination to control my life
with fear. To release this fear, I learn
to let go of what has been or what might
be. I focus only on this moment, and I
affirm that I am peace, I am love, I
am life. This brings me at one
with my Divine Spirit,
which is fearless.

I am fearless.

I am
secure
and fulfilled
in every
phase of
my life.

AFFIRM
DAILY.

just for this moment ...

I see insecurity as a fear of not succeeding in all I do. The security I seek is within. I totally surrender to my Divine Creator; then I will know I am safe and secure. I quickly release all sense of failure, for I know I can learn, step by step, ways to be absorbed in the totality of the power within. That power gives me faith, confidence, and happiness in all I do.

I am secure.

I live
in peace
and harmony,
and I accept
all beings
as kindred
spirits.

AFFIRM
DAILY.

just for this moment...

I see that the Divine Spirit
dwells within each and every being on
this planet. I see only the inner being. The
color of the skin and difference of cultures
matter not. The Spirit only desires all to live
in peace and harmony, and this comes
with acceptance of all that is. I learn
to see joy in all ideas, all religions,
and all beliefs, and I acquire
understanding and respect
of all beings.

I am loving.

I
am
a friend
to me
and to all
around
me.

AFFIRM
DAILY.

just for this moment ...

I see that people reflect me. I seek to have friendliness around, but first I must be a friend. I am happy to be friendly to all I meet and to see the beauty therein. I trust myself and fear no rejection. In giving love and friendliness to the world, my reward is peace and harmony. I glow in the knowledge that when I befriend me the Universe is a friend to me.

I am a friend.

I
drink
only
the sweet
nectar
of life,
which
is love.

AFFIRM
DAILY.

just for this moment ...

*I drink only the sweet
nectar of life, which is love.
I am created equal with all. I am
worthy of love, peace, and happiness,
for God intended it to be so. I am led to
ways that I can help myself and others be free
from the turmoil of drunkenness. I know
that step by step I am freed from the
need to punish myself. My Creator
only know love, and I am that
love. I choose to express it
and accept it into my
life right now.*

I am life.

I see
with the
eyes of love,
which recognize
only
harmony
everywhere.

AFFIRM
DAILY.

just for this
moment ...

I see perfection in all creation.
It is only the way I interpret things
that makes life seem to be in turmoil.
I choose to see the goodness, the kindness,
the beauty, and the simplicity all around
me. The love within wants me to see
and feel perfect always. I choose to
see with the eyes of love, which
is only recognizing order
everywhere.

I am synchronization.

I am
safe with
my sexuality,
for I am me
and I am
beautiful.

AFFIRM
DAILY.

just for this moment ...

I see that my bodily functions
are perfect right here and right now.
I see that to deny my sexuality is to deny
everything about me. The Divine Love within
is me, and I express that joyfully. I seek
not to be lustful but to be lifted in the
Spirit of God. In this Spirit, I behold
the miracle of my own being. I see
that I am an important part
of divine creation and that
the life is love within me.

I am me.

I am
under
divine
protection,
and I am always
at the right
place at the
right time.

AFFIRM
DAILY.

just for this moment ...

I recognize my fears; my beliefs attract into my life events that appear to be beyond my control. When I release those beliefs, I no longer attract accidents. I see all events as an experience for me to learn to lose all restrictions. God's love is no accident. It is always there and always will be. I now choose to change my perception to be in tune with the loving guiding force within. This enables me to be "in perfect control."

I am aware.

I see
a ray of
sunshine
in hope,
which brings
love to me
now.

AFFIRM
DAILY.

just for this moment ...

I choose to see life in a hopeful way. I do this by releasing all the expectations of myself. I live only in this moment, and I give thanks, for there is love in you, in me, and in the world. I see the power within teaching me that where there is hope there is life! I see a ray of sunshine in hope, which brings a glow to my heart. That glow reassures me that I am never alone, for it is the power within me.

I am hopeful.

I am
guided by
the inner
voice of
love, and
I make
decisions
easily.

AFFIRM
DAILY.

just for this moment ...

*I am still. I listen to the
voice within, which enables me to
release the fears and doubts. I now see
that all decisions are my teachers, and I
learn well. I am free of all limitations, as
the loving, wise voice within frees me
now of all fears. I learn to trust that
inner voice, which guides me
gently on my pathway
of life.*

I am guided.

I am
always
on the
winning
side of
life.

AFFIRM
DAILY.

just for this
moment ...

*I see that I cannot lose
anything that is mine by divine
right. I release all thoughts of lack,
for there is no lack in the Universe and
there is no lack in me. My life's requirements
are met abundantly, simply because I deserve
it. I now choose my divine birthright,
which is to live in abundance. I see
now that the love within will
release all limitations and
only guide me to my
perfect outcome.*

I am a winner.

I use
my gift
of life
with care, and I
perceive
everything
in love.

AFFIRM
DAILY.

just for this moment...

I see that I was created
in love. My perceptions have
been of pain or joy, turmoil or
peace, and I see that life has been
different for all. I look and see that
my purpose in life is to learn love. I
know my Creator breathed into me the
spirit of love, which is life for me, and life
is eternal. It is only my perception that
changes. I cherish my gift of life and
express it with love, peace, and
tenderness. I now dwell in
harmony, and my life's
purpose is fulfilled.

I am perception.

I am
led to the
almighty,
miraculous
power
of love.

AFFIRM
DAILY.

just for this
moment . . .

*I see that to have love in my
world, I need to love me. When
I learn to love and accept me, I can
then accept totally into my life loving
people and loving events. In the expansion
of my knowledge and understanding, I am led
to the almighty, miraculous power of love.
This is the life-giving essence within me.
This Divine Love is for me to
experience and rejoice in, for
it sets me free of burdens.*

I am Divine Love.

I sing
songs of
praise, and
I am
blessed in
every phase
of my
life now.

AFFIRM
DAILY.

just for this moment ...

I see that all experiences in
my life are moments of learning.
I give thanks to the Creator for my
life, for it has brought many rewards
of joy and happiness. I sing songs of praise,
and I am blessed in every phase of my
life now. My consciousness is lifted to
a state of gratitude, and I respect
every living thing. I fill this
moment with joy.

I am grateful.

I
observe
and accept
that all is
perfect
now.

AFFIRM
DAILY.

just for this moment ...

I learn to expand my
awareness, and I know
that everything is perfect
now. It was only my attitude
that made things seem imperfect
for me. I lift my consciousness, I lift
my perception, to a state of acceptance and
observation. I see perfection everywhere.
The Divine Spirit within wants me
to learn to love and be loved
unconditionally. That
is perfection.

I am perfect.

My
parents
love me, and
I choose
to love
them freely.

AFFIRM
DAILY.

just for this
moment ...
*I release all negative
thoughts and see the good
there has been. I was conceived
and born in love, and it is only my
perception that makes it seem otherwise.
All the actions, all the advice, and all the
discipline come because my parents love me.
I choose to love freely in the knowledge
that I accept their love as only they
can show it to me. I fill every
moment with love; then I see
how good it is knowing that
love has always been there.*

I love my parents.

I
release
all
barriers;
I express
myself
lovingly.

AFFIRM
DAILY.

just for this moment...

The walls of protection
around me crumble in love.
The wall I had created did not
allow love in or out! In learning to
love without conditions and expectations,
I know I am able to express myself easily
and lovingly. The Divine Spirit within
wishes me no harm, only peace and
harmony. I fill my soul, my being,
with joy, and I release all
barriers. I now
love openly.

I am loving openly.

I
love me
and my
Universe,
and I treat
all with
respect.

AFFIRM
DAILY.

just for this moment...

*I compare not, and I express
myself in a way comfortable for
me. I learn to understand myself
and those around me. I become aware
that there is joy in all I do, and I know
that this joy is the expression of my life. The
joy within delights all I meet, simply
because it is me. I accept me, as I
know I will expand my
understanding of loving
and being loved
without feeling
foolish.*

I am respect.

I am a
perfect
creation
of love,
and I am
beautiful.

AFFIRM
DAILY.

just for this moment ...

I release all hidden tensions, resentments, and discords, and I am free of all bondage. I now seek to nourish the Divine Spirit within, for then it nurtures me. I learn that the only comfort and security I need is within. Therefore I only eat and drink what my body requires to keep my body healthy. I accept the comfort of the love within and know that every day in every way my purpose in life is fulfilled.

I am beautiful.

I
now
choose
to have
complete
acceptance
of myself and
others.

AFFIRM
DAILY.

just for this moment ...

I see goals as something
I can work to achieve, but
I see expectations as limitations.
Where I "expect" success, the Spirit
does not; where I "expect" gain, the
Spirit does not; where I "expect" perfection,
the Spirit sees it as already perfect. I now
see that in having no expectations at all
I have everything right now! I see the
strength in unlimiting thoughts, for
the power within has no
expectations, only
gratitude of
what is.

I am acceptance.

I
love
myself
and totally
accept
myself.

AFFIRM
DAILY.

just for this moment...

I make no judgment of what
is right or wrong: therefore, there
is no need for punishment. I see the
love of God to be perfect in every way.
My life is a series of learning experiences,
and all decisions, judgments, and events were
not wrong but perfect for that moment.
I move through life easily, in the
knowledge that there is no need
to punish myself or others. I
change my perception to
loving myself tenderly.
I am at one with
my world.

I am love.

I
have
unshakable
faith
in the
power
within.

AFFIRM
DAILY.

just for this moment...

I see that "in love" there is nothing to fear. I break all patterns and beliefs of fear, for I wish only to dwell totally in love. I see the people and events I fear as something I can learn to overcome with love and acceptance. I expand my knowledge and understanding and release all fears, for love in life is eternally now.

I am faith.

The
power
within is
patient,
understanding,
and wise.

AFFIRM
DAILY.

just for this moment ...

*I fill this moment with love,
I breathe easily, knowing that "my"
way isn't necessarily the "only" way.
I release my frustrations in the knowledge
that everything is as it should be—perfect. I
learn to expand my awareness and free
myself from all fear. I learn love in
everything I do. The power within
is patient, understanding, and
wise. I now express patience
and understanding in
everything I say and
in everything I do.*

I am patient.

I
release
all my fears and
resentments;
they are
dissolved
in love.

AFFIRM
DAILY.

just for this moment...

I seek no revenge. I release
my fears and my resentments;
I see them dissolved in love. The
love within me is calming and does
not judge or condemn. I see now that
the Divine Spirit dwells in all, not just a
few; this enables me to give understanding,
compassion, and tenderness. The Divine
Love within is calming and gentle. I
choose to be in that calming
state of mind now.

I am calm.

I
forgive
and let go
of all
bitterness
now.

AFFIRM
DAILY.

just for this moment...

*I forgive. I release. I let go
all bitter feelings and breathe
easily. I breathe in the love of life
and see that I am the only one who
hurts me. My emotions of rejection that
I found unforgiving melt in the essence of love.
I now choose to be happy in the knowledge
of allowing myself to learn to love again
and set all bitterness free. The love
within gives continuously
with glee.*

I am gleeful.

I
rejoice
in the
knowledge
that the
Spirit is
life
eternal.

AFFIRM
DAILY.

just for this moment...

*I see the physical body fading
away to the nothingness from whence
it came. Death is not an end but merely
a beginning. In that knowledge, I rejoice
with love and celebration. I see that in God's
kingdom nothing dies, for life is eternal.
The Spirit moves on to spread love and
joy elsewhere. I let go of the fear of
death, for I now see it as a birth
of something wonderful. I give
thanks for the privilege
of life and living.*

I am free.

I
relinquish
all grudges,
and I am
free to
express
life
joyfully.

AFFIRM
DAILY.

just for this moment ...

I choose to dwell in peace
and love. I recognize that holding
a grudge is to criticize self and hurt
self, which will only lead to unhappiness.
I release all tension and breathe in easily the
free-flowing breath of life, which is love.
The Spirit within knows only peace
and forgiveness, and I choose
to have that now.

I am happiness.

I am
now in a
balanced,
peaceful
state of
mind.

AFFIRM
DAILY.

just for this moment ...

I seek no justice, for in the kingdom of heaven there is no judgment. There is no right, no wrong. It is only my beliefs that urge me to seek justice. The Divine Love within only knows peace and harmony. I now seek that peace and harmony and dwell therein. The law of love sees only balance, joy, and peace of mind. I am in that peaceful state of mind right now.

I am balanced.

All
children
are a joy.
We love
and grow
together.

AFFIRM
DAILY.

just for this moment...

I release quickly the expectations of conditional loving. I am me, and I am the best parent I can be. I learn quickly that every moment is special. I spend quality time, which is special time because I give that time in love— no conditions. This moment is a joy to behold, for we spend it together and it helps us to grow and learn love.

Children are perfect.

I
accept
myself
as a
perfect
creation
of love.

AFFIRM
DAILY.

just for this moment ...

*I accept the masculine and
feminine qualities in my physical
body and personality. I accept my
body as a perfect creation of God. My
choice is to be true to myself. I leave the
fight, the struggle, behind and enjoy life as
I am meant to, in peace and harmony. The love
and fulfillment I seek are within. I am
whole and complete right now in
the knowledge that the power
within has no preference of
sex—only love—and I give
thanks for that love.*

I am perfect.

My
Spirit
is free
and gentle,
and I express
freedom
now.

AFFIRM
DAILY.

just for this moment...

I see my Spirit just like a butterfly—gentle, unrestricted, and free. I happily learn that to place restrictions on myself is to stifle the grace, the beauty, and the freedom I am entitled to. I now choose to lift my perceptions above burdens and fill my Spirit with love. I rejoice in being free, and I enjoy life fully as it was meant to be, graciously.

I am freedom.

I learn
to obey
my loving
inner voice,
for it
guides me to
my highest
good.

AFFIRM
DAILY.

just for this moment ...

I see that the only
disobedience exists in
each individual's interpretation
of what "should" be. I do not expect
obedience from anyone else but myself.
In learning and expanding my awareness,
I see that all can hear the voice within.
It is my choice to follow that loving
guidance obediently, for it is for
my divine good.

I am obedience.

I allow
love into
my life,
and hatred
is dissolved
now.

AFFIRM
DAILY.

just for this moment ...

Hatred goes when I allow love
into my life. Everyone reflects what
I think of myself. When I allow this
love totally into my life, all feelings of
hatred, rejection, and lack of love disappear.
It is up to me now to choose to move
forward with new courage. That
courage is Divine Love and
releases all vulnerability,
for I am now free.

I am free.

I speak
love, peace,
and life into
my bones,
organs,
and body
now.

AFFIRM
DAILY.

just for this moment...

I see that disease and illness
have been created by my negative
thoughts and beliefs. I claim my divine
birthright of good health now. I feed my
physical body with nourishing foods; I feed
my spiritual body with loving thoughts
and words. I speak love, peace, and
life into my bones, my organs, and
my body, and I realize I am a
living temple of my Creator.
I bloom and flourish
in God's love

I am healthy.

I
have
loving
power to
control
my life.

AFFIRM
DAILY.

just for this moment ...

I see that the awe-inspiring
power within is all I need. I seek
not to change the world but me! When
I release this power within, I know I am
free, for every thought, word, and deed
uttered with love spreads gracefully
and easily. It is the power of
love that is almighty.

I am power.

I
release
my anger, and
I choose
to have
peace and
harmony.

AFFIRM
DAILY.

just for this moment...

I see that all my anger is in a balloon, and I send it far into the Universe, where it disappears and dissolves to nothingness. I now breathe easily, and I take into my being the breath of life, and I am free of anger. Anger only separates me from my divine right, the expression of love. I am now free to live life as God intended me to, peacefully and lovingly.

I am free.

I
release
all
embarrassment,
and I always
feel
joyful.

AFFIRM
DAILY.

just for this moment ...

I hear and listen only to the words spoken. I release all emotional attachments that make me feel humiliated. I learn to like and accept myself totally. Then I am able to express myself without guilt or shame. In recognizing the love within, I hear only words of happiness, fulfillment, and joy.

I am release.

I
dwell in
truth, and
that truth
is the perfect
balance
for me.

AFFIRM
DAILY.

just for this moment . . .

I see that the deception is in my comparisons of what is truth and what is not. I have a super intelligence within me, and I only deceive myself to think otherwise. This wisdom is the only truth for me, for it is simple, safe, sure, and fulfilling. I am alive in the knowledge that I dwell in truth and that truth is the perfect balance for me.

I am truth.

I
bring
acceptance,
love, and
worthiness
into my
life.

AFFIRM
DAILY.

just for this moment ...

I see that the only
person who victimizes
me is me. It is my feeling
of being unloved, unwanted, and
unworthy that attracts deception,
sacrifices, and injuries into my life.
I now lift my perception above hurt and
ridicule, for I now learn life is as beautiful
as I wish it to be. The truth and wisdom
within is all-encompassing, and I
grow in that wisdom of
perfection happily.

I am acceptance.

I
successfully
achieve all
things
with
ease.

AFFIRM
DAILY.

just for this moment...

I am alive, and that is no
failure. I see that in comparing
myself with others I feel a sense
of failure. When I look again, I see
that in trying I have succeeded, and
my successes are many. To breathe and
live life to the best of my ability is success
itself. I now choose to live every moment
in love, happiness, and contentment,
and I feel successful in everything
I do. When I am willing to
bring this into my life, my
Spirit is pleased in me.

I am success.

I am
relaxed, and I
flow
with
life
easily.

AFFIRM
DAILY.

just for this moment...

I choose not to force my will
onto others, for it is not my will
but thine that will be done. I do not
need to fight, struggle, and use force to
achieve love and peace. I center myself to
the God within and fight not. I accept
thy will of love and move through
life without resistance. God
shows me the only perfect
way for me, and I
surrender to that
peaceful state
now.

I am relaxed.

I
only have
thoughts
of joy and
love, and I see
perfection in
everything.

AFFIRM
DAILY.

just for this moment ...

I learn to love my body,
my thoughts, and my words.
I then know that I create the world
around me. The God within sees no
obscenities. I see my lack of understanding
as a hindrance to recognizing just how
powerful pure love can be. I know
I can learn this love and, in
turn, everything and
everybody.

I am pure.

I am a
beautiful
person,
worthy
of love and
happiness.

AFFIRM
DAILY.

just for this moment . . .

I give thanks, for the
depression will pass when
I dwell only on the beauty
around me. I choose to realize that
love comes from within—nowhere else.
I am a beautiful person worthy of love and
happiness, and I am not alone, for I know
the power within loves me. I see wonder
in me and all that encompasses me.
I see love in everything I do, for
that is what my Divine Spirit
knows is true. Joy is all
around, and I choose
to see it so.

I am happy.

I
have
trust
in the
Universe,
for it always
provides
abundantly.

AFFIRM
DAILY.

just for this
moment ...

I see everything will be as it should be, in its perfect time, space, and sequence. I choose to concern myself not with things that have been or might be. Instead, I choose to see the beauty and the joy in the moment with me. I learn to trust and listen to the still, quiet inner voice that guides me to my divine good.

I am trust.

Conclusion

There is really nothing new in what is being presented here, just my viewpoint. The challenge I throw to you is: Don't believe what I say; try it, and see what happens to you!

Above all, please be gentle with yourself, for the key is "never give up" and treat each moment as a new beginning. For with patience and quiet perseverance, we will all achieve the kingdom of heaven God promised.

I ask one favor of you: Please allow the part of you, the part of me, that is the Divine Spirit to reassure you that "just for this moment" love and peace *do* reign in your heart now.

Go in peace on your journey of fulfillment and know that your realization of complete love and happiness is only a moment away.

Yours in love and peace,

Carole Daxter

ABOUT THE AUTHOR

Carole is a Western Australian born and based clairvoyant, channeler, and personal development practitioner. A wife and mother of four, Carole experienced many traumatic events in her life that brought her to a crossroad—suicide or change?

Carole chose the latter and explored the reasons her life had become so unhappy. In her search for something better, studying metaphysics opened a happy, healthy new pathway.

Carole believes thoughts and spoken words are the most powerful tools at our fingertips. She has used affirmations daily in her growth work. Now, Carole shares, guides, and supports those who attend her courses. She has also written another book on affirmations called Love and Peace Through Affirmation *(also published by H J Kramer).*

In addition to offering personal development and healing courses, Carole and her husband Brian serve as Reiki therapists, spiritual counselors, and friends to all they meet.

*You can write to Carole Daxter at
P.O. Box 661
Kalamunda 6076
Western Australia*

COMPATIBLE BOOKS

FROM H J KRAMER INC

LOVE AND PEACE THROUGH AFFIRMATION
by Carole Daxter
*"Among the leaders in books that inspire and
expand human awareness."*—COLIN SISSON

WAY OF THE PEACEFUL WARRIOR
by Dan Millman
*A tale of transformation and adventure
. . . a worldwide best-seller.*

An Orin/DaBen Book
OPENING TO CHANNEL:
HOW TO CONNECT WITH YOUR GUIDE
by Sanaya Roman and Duane Packer, Ph.D.
*This breakthrough book is the first
step-by-step guide to the art of channeling.*

TALKING WITH NATURE
by Michael J. Roads
*"From Australia comes a major new writer
. . . a magnificent book!"*—RICHARD BACH,
Author, *Jonathan Livingston Seagull*

An Orin/DaBen Book
CREATING MONEY
by Sanaya Roman and Duane Packer, Ph.D.
This best-selling book teaches advanced manifestion techniques.

YOU THE HEALER: THE WORLD-FAMOUS SILVA
METHOD ON HOW TO HEAL YOURSELF AND OTHERS
by José Silva and Robert B. Stone
YOU THE HEALER *is the complete course in
Silva Method techniques presented in
a do-it-yourself forty-day format.*

MESSENGERS OF LIGHT:
THE ANGELS' GUIDE TO SPIRITUAL GROWTH
by Terry Lynn Taylor
*At last, a practical way to connect with the angels
and to bring heaven into your life.*

COMPATIBLE BOOKS

FROM H J KRAMER INC

THE EARTH LIFE SERIES
by Sanaya Roman, Channel for Orin
*A course in learning to live with joy,
sense energy, and grow spiritually.*

LIVING WITH JOY, BOOK I
*"I like this book because it describes the way I feel
about so many things."*—VIRGINIA SATIR

**PERSONAL POWER THROUGH AWARENESS:
A GUIDEBOOK FOR SENSITIVE PEOPLE, BOOK II**
"Every sentence contains a pearl . . ."—LILIAS FOLAN

**SPIRITUAL GROWTH:
BEING YOUR HIGHER SELF, BOOK III**
*Orin teaches how to reach upward to align with
the higher energies of the universe, inward to expand
awareness, and outward to engage in world service.*

JOURNEY INTO NATURE: A SPIRITUAL ADVENTURE
by Michael J. Roads
*An unforgettable book about humanity
as perceived through the eyes of nature.*

**SEVENFOLD PEACE: BODY, MIND, FAMILY,
COMMUNITY, CULTURE, ECOLOGY, GOD**
by Gabriel Cousens, M.D.
*"This book expands our awareness of the dimensions of peace
so that we can all work effectively to create a world at peace."*
—JOHN ROBBINS, Author, *Diet for a New America*

**JOY IN A WOOLLY COAT:
GRIEF SUPPORT FOR PET LOSS**
by Julie Adams Church
JOY IN A WOOLLY COAT *is about living with,
loving, and letting go of cherished animal friends.*

**EAT FOR HEALTH: FAST AND SIMPLE WAYS OF
ELIMINATING DISEASES WITHOUT MEDICAL ASSISTANCE**
by William Manahan, M.D.
"Essential reading and an outstanding selection."—LIBRARY JOURNAL